styleWORD

FASHION QUOTES FOR REAL STYLE

Stylist tips, tricks and motivation
to inspire your best dressed self!

SHARON HAVER

styleWORD
Fashion quotes for real style. Stylist tips, tricks and
motivation to inspire your best dressed self.

By
Sharon Haver

www.FocusOnStyle.com | www.StyleWordBook.com
team@focusonstyle.com

Copyright © 2016
Published by FocusOnStyle Press, New York, NY

Words, styling, art direction and photography by Sharon Haver
Assistant style direction by Naveed Hussan
Layout by www.TheBookProducer.com
Printed in the United States of America

ISBN 978-0-9974273-0-1

Connect with Sharon...

Visit Sharon's website at FocusOnStyle.com
Read her blog at FocusOnStyle.com/blog

Get Social with Sharon...

Twitter, Pinterest, Instagram, YouTube: @FocusOnStyle
Facebook: Sharon Haver – FocusOnStyle.com
LinkedIn: SharonHaver

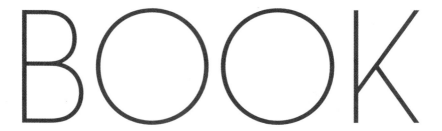

BOOK

Do you like gifts?

Me too!

In deepest appreciation for purchasing styleWord, *Fashion Quotes For Real Style*, I've created a special complimentary style companion to extend your style mentoring experience as my gift to you.

Bonus

Do you want it?

All you need to do is hop over to this web site to...

Claim Your Free Gift:

www.StyleWordBook.com/bonus

Enjoy!

Want to Quote a Quote?

You are welcome to share any of the individual quotes in this book IF you properly attribute them to Sharon Haver, FocusOnStyle.com and/or use the appropriate copyright ©Sharon Haver, FocusOnStyle.com.

Contents

About Sharon Haver

Sharon Haver is a New York based fashion and style expert, stylist, columnist, speaker, author and bootstrapping web entrepreneur.

You may know her as the founder of FocusOnStyle. com, where she has been sharing her fashion stylist tips online since 1999. As the creator of the C'est Chic Crash Course, she helps women think like a stylist and rule their own personal chic with her step-by-step style mentoring system based on her three decades in the style industry.

As a leading New York fashion stylist her work ran the gambit from styling Vogue covers with major jewels and couture clothes to making polyester sweats look great in ads so that you would actually want to wear them. Somewhere in between, she also styled catalogs and ads for top department stores, big name brands, magazine editorials, and the de rigeur celebrity and supermodel.

Sharon began her styling career because she felt a

boost in her self-confidence when she dressed well and wanted to share that with other women rather than the fantasy that she was creating on the photo set...

> "My heart is with the everyday woman,
> like you and me."

She brought her behind the scenes insider tips and tricks to women everywhere with her Focus on Style fashion advice column on the Scripps Howard News Service that was distributed to 400 newspapers each week.

The print column in combination with her B.B.A. degree in Marketing and entrepreneurial spirit lead the way for bootstrapping FocusOnStyle.com, now in its 17th year online, as your online style guide to can-do chic.... way before the job title "fashion blogger" was ever coined.

All this has brought her a wealth of media opportunities on the topics of fashion, style + success, ageless chic, lifestyle, marketing and entrepreneurism.

You can find her bio here: FocusOnStyle.com/sharon

Welcome To Your Cheat Sheet To Style!

#styleWORDBook

Sometimes I'm guilty of skimming books to get to the meat. Especially personal development books.

So if you're like me, I created styleWORD just for you...
it's the ultimate cheat sheet to upgrade your look in the shortest amount of time.

Like rapid time. Like short attention span social media time.

You don't even need to read the post. Or listen to the interview. Or even read the question that the column addresses. Just get to the takeaway quote.

I culled through about a thousand-ish of my top posts on FocusOnStyle.com. And even earlier ones from my fashion advice column. I pulled pithy passages from some of my interviews. And got all creative and updated and added to my arsenal of speedy style and fashion advice.

I want you to walk your walk… with that certain bounce…. the kind you get from having the air of self-confidence… the one that comes from knowing that you have it going on.

And I walk my walk as well.

I styled all the photos in this book. Used my own wardrobe. My own home accessories. Did my own hair and makeup. Everything. Just so you can see that if I can do it, so can you. Without crazy preparation. Without obsessing. Without fuss. Once you get a handle on your style, it begins to be instinctual. You'll see.

It's just as easy to make an ugly choice as it is to make a fantastic choice… so why settle?

StyleWORD is your stylist express for high-impact style snippets + fashion advice that gets to the point. Let's get started!

Love, peace and style,

Sharon

#styleWORDBook

Beauty Inside + Out

Style should always
APPEAR EFFORTLESS,
no matter what it takes.

No one should be **without** a good tweezer and a bottle of hair conditioner.

.....

Colored sunglasses may be like **makeup** for your face but dark sunglasses are forever chic.

.....

The best beauty tip **EVER**: Shape those eyebrows!

Find good lighting. Bask underneath it. Always. (wink)

.....

You are **THE ONE** who needs to feel comfortable about your appearance first, then there's no need to worry about what other's say.

.....

There's no better quick fix makeover than a *great haircut* to look modern and renewed.

Women who forget to make the effort in their overall beauty regime wind up looking terribly dated and dull. Yawn.

.....

Perfume should never precede you nor linger in a room – only dogs need to leave their scent.

.....

With the right skills & attitude every woman can turn "it" on and stand out from the crowd in **EVERY** stage of her life.

Use makeup & your imagination to create a sense of fantasy, rebellion and edge beyond fashion when the mood strikes... but by all means do not let your makeup overwhelm you. Same goes for tattoos.

.....

There's no excuse not to adapt a fast, five-minute, **natural makeup** routine that can get you out of the house looking refreshed every day.

All the makeup in the world won't take the place of a good skincare regime. Take care of the skin you are in.

.....

Looking gorgeous is mindset, plus some calculated effort to make the most of what you've got… **know yourself** to make the best of yourself.

.....

Sexiness should be in the subtleties.

Never say

Never...

Don't beat yourself down about being the odd one out on fashion and beauty. Develop the mindset to grow.

.....

Beauty is how **YOU** see yourself.

.....

Relish your physical attributes and let go of what holds you back.

.....

Make beauty a priority.

You don't need to hire a glam squad to look great. You just need to **take charge**. Let's get going!

.....

Looking gorgeous & living beautifully doesn't have an expiration date!

.....

True beauty comes from the inside but a skincare regimen + a little makeup lets it shine.

Never underestimate the *power* of a well-rimmed eye.

.....

Kisses, not lipstick, should linger… Matte that baby down!

.....

CELEBRATE the beauty of **YOU**!

Find **joy** in your reflection.

.....

Understand your nuances.

.....

Spotlight your strengths.

.....

SNAP, be ready for your close-up!

The major purpose of a makeover is to make you feel better about yourself, not to look like someone else.

Radiate your best self!

.....

Tomorrow is more beautiful than yesterday.

.....

Red lipstick is a 24/7 face brightener. Who says a bold lip is limited to the night?

It's not *her* style that counts,
it's **YOURS** that matters!

.....

Be true to yourself to believe
in yourself.

.....

Incorporate the power of
personality!

*Look in the mirror.
See what features you
like and what features
are less pleasing to
you. Rather than
covering up what you
don't like, **enhance**
what you like.*

#styleWORDBook

Style Motivation

There are no **cookie-cutter** rules to style.

.....

You can't find style when your mind is closed.

.....

Taste doesn't cost a thing!

.....

Comfort can be found in the right pair of 3″ heels.

No one should **TELL** you how to dress, but they can guide you.

.....

Think about your day ahead and dress to make the most of it.

.....

Take two extra minutes to look good, take five minutes to look great, 20 will **rock** their world!

Add color as a wardrobe **accent** but not as wardrobe maker.

.....

No one is above having style. Funny how the people who think they are look like sh*t.

.....

Better to try a new style and fail rather than to be stuck in a fashion rut. **B.O.R.I.N.G.**

*Gorgeous clothes will **NOT** turn you into a beauty. You must **BELIEVE** that you're beautiful — inside and out — to truly be a knock-out.*

Never skimp on shoes or a bag (people form impressions about their quality).

.....

Don't mind a bit of edge, that's what makes it all so interesting!

.....

If you look like you gave up hope on your appearance, you look like you gave up hope about yourself.

The secret of **timeless chic** is easy, fuss-free proportions that are not only right for the present, but right for the future.

.....

Once you have everything down pat as what *not* to do, focus on what you can realistically manage to be at ease in your personal elegance.

If it's been awhile since you have had some sexy style moments, be cautious not to look desperate and overdo it.

.....

A closet full of gorgeous neutrals alone does not always make for a synergistic wardrobe – it's all about **balancing proportions** so that what you have works in harmony.

Take a good look at yourself and be proud that you know you look the best you can that day.

.....

The only thing you can **control** is yourself. Dress accordingly.

.....

Be your own trendsetter. Always strive to be ahead of the curve.

When all else fails, think like a stylist and go for **something unexpected.**

.....

Use bling as an accent rather than drown yourself in death by diamanté.

.....

Understand the fine line between **modern** and **trendy**... stay on top of the first, and sprinkle in a bit of the second.

Fashion magazines don't portray reality, they show you how to alter fantasy so use editorial as your **launch point** to self-expression rather than copycat what you see in magazine pages.

.....

Just think of how interesting and more varied your wardrobe choices can be when you rework what you already own!

If you're on a strict budget, shy away from **super-trendy** items that will be out of style in a quick fashion minute. Same goes for once you passed your 40th birthday.

.....

Money doesn't buy style, it only makes it easier to listen to a salesperson.

.....

Become a fan of the **high-low**. Blend budget-friendly trends with quality basics for sizzling style.

They say, don't go to the super-market on an empty stomach, well, don't go shopping for a new wardrobe **totally clueless**.

.....

Style shouldn't have an expiration date.

.....

Make the effort to immerse yourself in style until you actually "get" the difference between what is blah and what is stunning.

Looking great is not only the best revenge, it's the best self-confidence booster!

.....

Add global to your local, the internet makes the world your backyard. Dress for it.

.....

It's all about can-do chic!

.....

Simple. Perfect. Style.

Don't whine. Don't wish. Make **today** your day to start looking fabulous.

.....

Style is *not* about the price tag.

.....

Staying modern is the best revenge!

.....

Shortcuts equal shortcomings.

Looking great & stylish is about the sum of its parts. It's not about individual items but how those unique items work together to create the total package of you.

Intentionally or not, we have all suffered from the crimes of fashion to some degree... don't kill yourself, laugh it off and move on.

.....

You don't need an oversized budget to have style, **just some imagination** and the understanding of what works on you.

Sometimes the outfit makes the memory.

.....

We should always attempt to dress in a way that makes us feel our best. When we **feel great**, we **look great**.

.....

Fashion is one of the few quick-change pleasures you can experience.

Liberate the fuglies out of your closet... there's a hipster at a thrift store somewhere waiting to pounce on those fuchsia cowboy boots.

.....

The best way to choose a core wardrobe is to put your lifestyle in a suitcase. Hone in on what you need to wear for a make-believe 5-day trip and make those essentials your wardrobe basics.

Admonish the phobia that you never look "right," and learn to do something about it.

.....

Make the most of what you've got by mastering fashion stylist skills to **be the "celebrity" in your own life**.

.....

Style is what you absorb from everything around you and how you subtly incorporate into your life.

Don't resolve to style. Evolve to style.

.....

You can't find style when your mind is closed. Get inspired!

.....

Your fashion shouldn't own you. You should own your style.

.....

Anyone can learn great style. It comes with a trained eye and patience.

Broaden your shopping horizons.

.....

It's all in the mix!

.....

Glamour is the **extra something** to make you twinkle.

.....

Saying no to excess is saying yes to white space... and that's exactly what you need to forge ahead, in style.

Strive to find the pleasure in getting dressed.

.....

Being confident in your style choices frees you up to have time to LIVE!

.....

Your dress is only one part of your busy life, make it seamless.

.....

Balance in the **unexpected**.

Curate. Edit.

Cultivate.

Yes, **WE** see your shoes. And they tell quite the story… so you best make it interesting.

.....

Stop hanging on to old clothes for the sake of it.

.....

Those who don't think that the color black is chic are the few who don't know how to wear it well.

.....

Obsessive coordination is boring.

Giving up on looking modern is just giving in to looking dowdy. And *that* will certainly pile years on to your appearance.

.....

Start simple and build from there. But **never scrimp** on staples, they are the pieces that make *any* wardrobe work.

.....

Rules are for fools when it comes to fashion. Once you know what you're doing, you'll be winging it!

Every time you feel frustrated shopping, just **think of those wishing they had your problem**. Suck it up for style… imagine that the better you are at editing what you need, the less you have to shop.

.....

Avoid being caught in a fashion rut because you're **afraid to experiment** with something new. Evolve!

.....

Style shouldn't be complicated.

It's easier to stay on top of editing your wardrobe if your closet is **organized**.

.....

Be open to trying new things to experiment with your personal style.

.....

Ease into updating like a woman on a mission.

.....

Use your comfort zone as a launch point to style… then **challenge yourself** to soar!

At a certain point in your life, you start to understand that the only opinion that really counts about how you look is your own. Educate yourself.

.....

There are a couple of ways to look at Fashion Week. You could go crazy wild with a total shift of silhouettes or you could find familiar shapes **tweaked into something fresh** yet not quite a dramatic shift from what you may already own.

I like the latter. So should you.

When it comes to updating your style, the self-confidence *really* needs to come from within.

.....

A subtle touch of **unexpected unfussiness** instantly ups your cool factor.

.....

Pulling off an the unexpected in just the right way is the epitome of effortless chic.

Forever Chic

A well-fitting black turtleneck should be a staple in every wardrobe.

·····

Lasting impressions are formed upon initial impact. (Make it your best!)

·····

SHEEP OR CHIC? Follow your personal style *not* the "It Girl" of the moment.

If you're not sure if something is flattering on you, **stick with your gut** and try something else.

.....

Explore your personal style and constantly tweak your look to stay modern.

.....

True style is about the harmony of how you put it all together.

Streamlined, timeless, and elegant style works well in any economy. So dress rich, it's a no brainer!

.....

Plaid shirts are like the **comfort food of fashion**, so just like mashed potatoes enjoy them but don't over do it!

.....

Looking good is more than a good dress, it's how you pull it all together.

One of the secrets French women have to looking chic is a tailor.

Clean, chic and minimalist styles that are unfussy, easy to wear, and most importantly timeless yet modern should be the **FOUNDATION OF ANY WARDROBE** anywhere.

.....

Who is your fashion icon? Someone famous or a friend or family member? Take note of what stands out about her style so you can tweak to to best suit you!

Put your spin on normal and master it to superb… that's the secret to great everyday style.

.....

Simple elegance worn in the right way with the right touch that flatters will always endure.

.....

Style is about looking gorgeous, fabulous and confident, *without* an expiration date.

Never leave the house dressed as someone else – unless it's Halloween.

.....

It's not the dress that walks into the room first. It's the woman wearing the dress who gets noticed... that's priceless.

.....

The right fitting black turtleneck belongs in *every* wardrobe.

Don't be bogged down by the year you were born or the lack of resources you have as with the right skills & attitude *every* woman can turn "IT" on to stand out from the crowd at *every* stage of her life.

.....

Great style doesn't have to be expensive!

.....

Tweak it to make it your own. Always.

Looking professional and chic always involves a bit of timeless elegance.

.....

Ageless style is **NOT** about a number; it's about how **YOU** look.

.....

What is tacky on someone young, will be even more tacky on someone older.

The purity of a well-cut piece with the accent of something special is more elegant and chic than a mish-mash of overdone and competing elements could ever be.

.....

If someone else dresses you, your look will never be a part of you, just a reflection of how "they" see you. **True style comes from within yourself** so that you can honestly feel at ease with yourself and in your outfit.

Realize that the same classic boxy suit or conservative tailoring that looks powerful, pulled together and fresh on someone under 25 makes a woman more mature look like a frump.

Just because a certain style is shown to be in style, doesn't mean it's **appropriate** for you.

.....

At a certain age, super-refined pieces serve you better than fussy pieces.

.....

You **never** want to look like you went **all** out. Keep things looking simple and effortless (even if it took you just a few extra minutes to pull together).

Looking ageless is looking great. Period. It's *nothing* to do with the year we were born.

.....

Confidence is chic.

.....

Run like heck from being trapped in the geezer ghetto of styleless fashion unless you want to appear looking older and duller. Feh.

.....

Don't give in to dowdy.

Release the belief that you must follow every trend to be fashionable.

.....

ASPIRE to be the best you can be at *that* very moment.

.....

NEVER FEEL encumbered by your age. Be free from restrictions to anything other than what is flattering for you right now.

Even if you are casual, your clothes need to say "I get it" with the right pieces.

.....

Appear powerful, confident, and modern to look relevant.

.....

The best way to not look old is to **stop** dressing like an old lady.

.....

Wear only what's worthy of your discerning stylish eye.

If you are unsure, ask yourself if it's one of The Three C's of Style: Classy, Chic + Cool.

Looking classic means you will **NEVER** look dated in a photograph and always have the right aura of style & luxe.

.....

Invest in black.

.....

It's the right touch of sophisticated accents that creates that special yin and yang to look confident, timeless and sexy.

.....

Hang onto your youthful spirit.

Less is more when the elements
are right.

.....

Bland, Frumpy + Dated is **NOT**
an option.

.....

Never wear vintage as it was
worn the first time.

.....

Just because something is
"in" does mean it should be in
YOUR wardrobe.

Be the **STYLIST** of **YOUR** own style!

.....

Dump the frump!

.....

Knowing when to say **NO** is **very** chic.

.....

Too much, too many, too-too are **TOO MANY THINGS**.

.....

Discover the ease of simplicity.

Trust your own sense of style.

.....

Appropriate is what works for you today.

.....

It's okay to take a day off from style, but **NEVER** a lifetime.

.....

Accept and grow.

.....

Less is more, when it's **RIGHT**.

There's no need to be so overdone that you look like you were sideswiped by the accessories van.

You don't have to prove how much you own only that you know how to ***edit what you have.***

Pretty, Sexy + Chic = **YOU**.

.....

Neutrals exude elegance.

.....

Vivid color is best as an accent.

.....

Don't lose yourself in the noise
of glaring colors.

.....

Classic shades are sophisticated.

Grow up! Juvenile details and baby colors only make you look older.

.....

It's not about designer labels, it's more about **how the clothes flatter you**.

.....

Youth doesn't guarantee a hot bod, but age certainly should shine some wisdom: Flatter your figure and *make the most* of what you've got!

Once you start taking clothing too seriously, you lose all sense of style and become a fashion victim. And boring.

.....

No wardrobe can be versatile, functional, and chic without a **solid base**.

.....

Age has nothing to do with physical shape, spirit, or the desire to move forward and stay vital.

Great *personal style* is about understanding yourself, what makes you tick and what you want to project.

.....

Think of your belt as an accessory or a jewel and you won't need anything else.

.....

Every wardrobe craves those certain perennially fashionable items that no matter what become our go-to staples.

Grown-up girls know that well-cut clothes with clean lines are better than fussy layers and crazy prints.

.....

Almost no one ever wears what is actually shown on the runway. But everyone should open up to its influence. A nuance here. A trend there. **Rethink** how you get dressed every day with a healthy dose of catwalk inspiration.

.....

It's all about adapting.

#styleWORDBook

Fabulous Fit

Don't condemn a style just because it doesn't work on your figure... **ADAPT**!

.....

You don't need a lot of fashion to have style, just a few well-cut pieces.

.....

Well-fitting neutrals are the chicest core wardrobe.

.....

Dark colors are more slimming, but nothing beats a **GOOD FIT**.

Shoes need to both look good and be comfortable – one cannot have the other.

·····

Forget about the year you were born. Dress for the physical shape you are in today!

·····

Follow the **natural curve** of your body – flatter the spots that are not so perfect + accentuate your more positive attributes.

Few people look great in every-thing they try on. Those who do, simply know how to dress for their body shape.

.....

Understand your **shape** and dress for it.

.....

Collect the "if only it was a *little*... smaller, longer, shorter, tighter, fuller" items from your closet and take them to the tailor, once and for all!

Avoid too-clingy jersey fabrics that "grab" you in the wrong places. Okay, you can look like you have more rolls than Kaiser if you want to. Just kidding (not), opt for fabric that **graze** your body rather than grab or try micro layering featherweight pieces to avoid the bulge.

.....

Selecting the right fit is a job onto itself. Apply for the position!

Don't forget that it's not about how much something costs as much as it is about how something **fits** you and **flatters** your figure.

On the same theme, never wear anything that *looks* cheap. Price is perspective.

.....

When the tailor can't help, off to the donation bin it goes.

Purchase what flatters you today and not what you think you will shrink into next month.

Rather than feeling sorry for yourself about packing on 5+ pounds select silhouettes cut for your body.

.....

No matter what size you are or how busy you are, spending **a couple of extra minutes** getting ready will always help boost your self-confidence and style in an instant.

.....

Fit to flatter!

It's amazing how you can fake extravagance when something fits just so.

.....

Understand the power of the right fit.

.....

Honor your body.

.....

A well-fitting bra is a necessity.

.....

The right size is the size that *fits* you.

There's nothing easier than styling the right white T-shirt. Top it off with your favorite jacket, add a flirty neckerchief and suddenly your otherwise better than basic jeans are polished and statement making.

Wear what you feel confident wearing and use the mirror as your **BEST FRIEND**.

.....

There's no need to conform to one particular style all the time, simply understand the harmony in your total outfit.

.....

The more rigged you need to be to look great, the less comfortable you'll be. And that shows.

When you are in tune with your shape, you can eyeball a garment and instantly ascertain **whether or not** it will look good on you.

.....

Discover the styles that shape your wardrobe into a figure flattering asset. You will see how much easier **shopping** will be!

.....

The shape of the heel of your shoe should compliment the shape of your leg.

The bottom line is: Does it look good **TO** you and **ON** you?

.....

Accept the body you have and make the most of what you've got to **FEEL GREAT** about yourself.

.....

Clothing should act like a second layer to your flesh. Let it emphasize what you want to highlight and camouflages what you want to detract.

Always dress confidently + proportionately for the shape that you are in **TODAY**, whatever your size.

.....

Not every designer or brand is cut the same. Make the effort to find a line that's scaled for your shape. Go with it for your core wardrobe... let's search for basics!

Look for details that show off your figure in the most flattering way!

.....

Confidence is contagious! Look like a woman who knows what flatters her figure and personal style.

.....

Any style can be tweaked to look great on you.

.....

Consider what enhances your lines.

Do you want ageless allure? Forget about the year you were born and dress for the physical shape you are in today.

.....

Know the skin you are in. Accept it or make the effort to modify it.

.....

Mix and match and explore unique colours and shapes and look at fashion from a different angle.

The fit of the most elegant and flattering clothing has a lot to do with your **TOTAL** body shape rather than a specific area that you feel self-conscious about.

.....

A modern, well-cut matched or unmatched suit is one of the most versatile additions to your wardrobe and truly something worth investing in.

#styleWORDBook

Living in Your Elegance

Everyone has a **BAD** fashion day (it's a lifetime of **BLAND** fashion that's worrisome).

.....

The only eye that matters is **YOURS**. Make sure it's well-trained!

.....

Trust in your gut rather than flock with the fad.

.....

YOU are genius!

There are plenty of fashion trends that only look great on the young + skinny and simply look juvenile on the rest of us. Wrong place. Wrong time. Know when to say bye-bye.

Make the most of what you've got!

.....

Your story is your life so why borrow what someone else presents to you?

.....

Live a first-person life rather than in the shadow of your tribe.

.....

Be **at ease** in your presence.

Having someone to inspire you is paramount to manifesting your own personal abundance.

.....

There's a bit of the "Emperor's New Clothes" to pulling off something daring – if you **believe**, 'they' will believe it too.

.....

Experiment, play, and edit until you discover that secret something that makes style *personal* on you.

Fashion Math: Style is the amalgamation of the sum of its parts and not the collection of a batch of hit and miss items.

.....

The fact that you are asking for pointers means you have more of a style clue than you give yourself credit for (wink).

Many women —
particularly ones in their
twenties — get caught up
in a trend-by-numbers
way of dressing. Stop it.
It's boring, redundant,
and totally un-unique.
There, I made up a new
word for you!

Pluck up the courage to abandon those pigeonholing labels and **BE** yourself.

.....

Abundant style makes the most of what you've got so you don't waste a fortune playing dress up. It guides you to overflow with possibilities *without* feeling like you have a full closet and nothing to wear.

.....

Life is your inspiration board.

How you look is all relative to who else is in the room but how confident you feel about your appearance is what counts.

.....

Find the abundance in the exponential possibilities of **YOU**.

.....

Embrace what **inspires** you.

.....

Defy the naysayers.

*Style isn't about worrying about what you **CANNOT** wear but being aware of what you **CAN** wear.*

Reset yourself to evolve to a
better you.

·····

Invest in **YOUR** style.

·····

Style is about looking right,
feeling confident (and
creating the visual impression
of someone who can knock
it out of the park).

What to wear? How to wear it? Style is the confidence of knowing you've got it going on.

.....

Know how to turn **IT** on when **YOU** want to!

.....

Get stuck in the unique minutiae of **YOU**, not *her*!

It's about creating rather than copying.

.....

Be a genuine **YOU** rather than an imitation of someone else.

.....

Put your spin on normal and master it to superb.

.....

Don't follow, **finesse**.

Being in tune with your style means less stress. When you are confident you can effortlessly improvise getting dressed rather than panic that you have nothing to wear.

Look like you have arrived, not like you're still waiting for the bus.

.....

Make your personal pavement your red carpet!

.....

Don't buy clothes that **look good** on someone else.

.....

Keep the theatrics down + the sophistication up.

Your potential is **unstoppable**!

.....

Enjoy your reflection!

.....

Don't complicate it. Every outfit should have one focal point – not a million distracting elements screaming for attention.

.....

Trust yourself.

STYLE is a lot like *COOKING*. Start with the freshest ingredients for the most delicious results.

Look rich in your distinctive genius!

.....

Dress down with dignity!

.....

If you look like you tried too hard,
YOU tried too hard.

.....

The abundance of your presence
is limitless.

Wear glasses like you mean it! Be bold. Be proud. Be modern. (And give a good stomp to drugstore skinny readers and wireless frames unless you want to look 15 years older.)

Leave a little to the imagination, it's so much more alluring than baring too much.

.....

You should be looked at as being beautiful and ageless rather than what you can pull off at that age.

.....

Explore, experiment, and evolve. It's just clothes.

I hate any divisive rule when it comes to what you should or should not wear, yet there is **ONE** rule that says it all: never give up on common sense!

.....

Don't overthink style! Go with your gut – your first fashion choice is almost always the right choice.

.....

Feel good about who you are. No matter how fabulous your wardrobe is, it's still just clothing.

Project an air of self-confidence and poise. What you're wearing will suddenly look better.

.....

Wear whatever makes you feel good about you. For that matter, find a companion who does the same (wink).

.....

Modify trends to remain modern and understand your fashion limits.

Focus on what **YOU** find interesting.

.....

Everyone has a different approach to fashion. There is no one modus operandi to style other than being **authentic** to yourself.

.....

Make an effort to be present in how you present yourself, even when no one is looking.

Style key wardrobe pieces for the many moments in your life without having to water down your true sense of personal style.

.....

Break free from the rock you're living under and **open your eyes** to the visual world around you.

.....

Pulling yourself together – when you need to – is much the same for your style as it is for your lifestyle.

Inspiration is everywhere! Open your eyes and make the world your launch point to style!

#styleWORDBook

Brand You

You are your best product so **PACKAGE YOURSELF** to soar!

.....

Be passionate about you!

.....

The right clothes will make you feel self-confident (the wrong clothes will chip away at your self-esteem).

.....

Know your audience & dress appropriately!

Always remember to dress like you've made **IT**, whether you have or have yet to reach your dream.

·····

Be altruistic in your expertise and humble in your shortcomings.

·····

Effectiveness comes through the confidence of personal mastery rather than the parroting of peers.

Own it, not in the sense that you dumped the last revolving credit card payment on that outfit but more that YOU believe in you. And you believe in how fantastic it looks on YOU.

Have the self-confidence to know that you are amazing and so will everyone else.

.....

When we feel confident about our appearance we exude a wonderful aura of **triumph**.

.....

You can be the best you can and make the most of what you've got, if you open your mind and make the effort to let the possibilities happen.

Style subtly penetrates your being from wherever you are.

.....

Your personal brand is more than a pretty dress. It's how **everything fits together** as one gorgeous package!

.....

Your story is your life so why borrow what someone else presents to you? Really, why?

Package your personality rather than wrap it in someone else's.

.....

You are the face of your brand.

.....

Looking dated or giving the wrong impression is an instant turn off.

.....

Style your personal brand like you mean it: savvy, chic & approachable.

Be present in your presence.
Even when no one else is
looking.

.....

Have a style awakening!

.....

Style is more than just what
you wear, but how you present
yourself as a whole.

If you look pulled together, you'll be perceived the same way.

.....

Want a quick **ego boost**? Wear a great pair of heels!

.....

Always move forward to avoid falling into a rut.

*If you suddenly realize that how you presented yourself **BEFORE** has nothing to do with how you want to be perceived **NOW**, it's time for style **TRANSFORMATION**.*

Want to create an instant great first impression? Opt for the best quality you can afford even if it's an accent or a major thrift shop find.

.....

Awareness is *always* the first step to action but what follows is the first step to the solution.

.....

Dress the part!

#styleWORDBook

Business Style + Success

If you do it every day, learn to do it right. Like getting dressed!

.....

Take the Style Express by dressing the part of **where you want to be**, not where you are.

.....

If you still look like your high school graduation picture – from 1982 – it is truly **NOT** a good thing.

.....

Invest in yourself.

What you wear is a form of self-expression; make sure you are expressing the right image at the right time. Avoid sending mixed messages.

You need to **OWN YOUR LOOK** if you want to be taken seriously as a credible professional.

.....

There is absolutely no reason to look boring, unless you intentionally want to be perceived as the human yawn.

.....

Don't ever forget to dress for yourself first, and the rest will follow.

.....

Awareness is omnipotent.

What you wear in your business is an extension of how you dress every day.

.....

Life isn't an audition – **dress the part**!

.....

To be thoughtfully present in your presence is an internal process based on what inspires you, not what you outsource to someone else to do for you.

.....

It's hard to take a slob seriously.

In business, have respect for others by how you present yourself, it demonstrates your own self worth.

.....

Allow yourself to succeed in your style, just as you want to succeed in your business.

.....

Social media makes it easy to think that everyone else has a perfect life full of showy things. But is it true? Don't be a second-rate copy of a fake thing when you can be a first-rate version of yourself!

Pick pieces that reflect your personality rather than what "they" think is right. Just don't go crazy and look like the purple people eater if you want to be taken seriously.

Appearing office appropriate for the type of business that you are in is paramount but know how to stand out in the right way.

.....

Don't think of your business suit as blah – with a little imagination it can be your most **chic + versatile** piece in your closet!

.....

The best **personal brand** you can create is an honest, polished version of yourself.

Are you *really* ready? You spend time + effort on your professional development but skimp on the most crucial step – how you present yourself! Be ready to look the part!

.....

What you wear is your story. Not someone else's. Own it.

.....

Be present in your presence when you want to make your mark!

Never outsource your style! If you don't know how to dress yourself and you hire a personal stylist to dress you, you are just putting a Band-Aid on the problem. True style is knowing how to pull **YOURSELF** together, not having someone to do it for you.

.....

Life transitions can be just the signal you need to wake up your style!

*Dress how you want
to be perceived!*

Resources from Sharon Haver

FocusOnStyle.com

www.FocusOnStyle.com

FocusOnStyle is where I freely share my stylist tips to help you decipher the fashion code and get closer to *your* best self every day.

Become An Insider

www.FocusOnStyle.com/insiders

Be part of the free FocusOnStyle Community and be privy to special resources and information that I only share with my Insiders… stay in the loop and don't miss one very stylish thing!

The C'est Chic Crash Course

www.cest-chic.me

Looking pulled together shouldn't be agonizing. I created the style system to help you look your best every day. Grown up ladies know that it's not about being trendy but cultivating the ageless allure of C.H.I.C.™.

Style Mentoring Menu

www.FocusOnStyle.com/style-mentoring

Let's get close up + personal.... I've created a selection of services for you to learn what it takes to easily pull yourself together with the confidence to make the most of what you've got.

NOTES...